||||||||||||||||||||||||||||||||||||
I0087426

A CourseGuide for

A Survey
of the
New Testament

Robert H. Gundry

ZONDERVAN
ACADEMIC

ZONDERVAN ACADEMIC

A CourseGuide for A Survey of the New Testament

Copyright © 2019 by Zondervan

ISBN 978-0-310-11118-4 (softcover)

Requests for information should be addressed to:
Zondervan, *3900 Sparks Dr. SE, Grand Rapids, Michigan 49546*

Printed in the United States of America

CONTENTS

Introduction

Welcome to *A CourseGuide for A Survey of the New Testament*. These guides were created for formal and informal students alike who want to engage deeper in biblical, theological, or ministry studies. We hope this guide will provide an opportunity for you to grow not only in your understanding, but also in your faith.

How to Use This Guide

This guide is meant to be used in conjunction with the book *A Survey of the New Testament* and its corresponding videos, *A Survey of the New Testament Video Lectures*. After you have read each chapter in the book and watched the accompanying video lesson, the materials in this guide will help you review and assess what you have learned. Application-oriented questions are included as well.

Each CourseGuide has been individually designed to best equip you in your studies, but in general, you can expect the following components. Most CourseGuides begin every chapter with a "You Should Know" section, which highlights key terminology, people, and facts to remember. This section serves as a helpful summary for directing your studies. Reflection questions, typically two to three per chapter, prompt you to summarize key points you've learned. Discussion questions invite you to an even deeper level of engagement. Finally, most chapters will end with a short quiz to test your retention. You can find the answer key to each quiz at the bottom of the page following it.

For Further Study

CourseGuides accompany books and videos from some of the world's top biblical and theological scholars. They may be used independently, or in small groups or classrooms, offering quality instruction to equip students for academic and ministry pursuits. If you would like to engage in further study with Zondervan's CourseGuides, the full lineup may be viewed online. After completing your studies with *A CourseGuide for A Survey of the New Testament*, we recommend moving on to *A CourseGuide for A Survey of the Old Testament* and *A Course-Guide for Four Portraits, One Jesus*.

CHAPTER 1

Intertestamental and New Testament Historical Background

You Should Know

- The Greco-Macedonian military leader, Alexander the Great, brought Greek culture and language throughout the Mediterranean and near East. Greek culture left an indelible mark on the eastern Mediterranean world. Hellenism was not only part of Gentile society, but also a contentious part of Judaism.

- Palestine's location between Syria (Seleucids) and Egypt (Ptolemies) put it in between two great empires which had its advantages and disadvantages.

- Israel, after coming back from Babylonian exile, had adapted to life without the temple cult through its emphasis on the study of Torah, prayer, and strict adherence to the Law.

- The Romans eventually eclipsed the Greek empire, and in 63 BC they overtook Jerusalem. This paved the way for a series of rulers that remained loyal to Rome, while attempting to placate the native Jews.

- Intertestamental history: "the four hundred silent years"; the period between the end of Old Testament history and the start of New Testament history

- Hellenization: the spread of Greek culture, including especially the Greek language, so as to mix with other cultures

- Septuagint: a translation of the Old Testament from Hebrew into Greek

- Pentateuch: the first five books of the Old Testament, traditionally ascribed to Moses: Genesis, Exodus, Leviticus, Numbers, and Deuteronomy

- Bar Kokhba: a man by the name of Simon Bar Kosiba whom Rabbi Akiba believed to be the Messiah, and who led a revolt against the Roman empire in AD 135

- AD 70: destruction of Jerusalem and the temple by the Romans

Reflection Questions

1. Choose a prophet who lived during the Babylonian Exile (ex. Ezra, Malachi, Haggai, etc.): What are the problems he deals with, and what are the expectations of him and of the Jews of that time?

2. Judaism at this time was divided into the Hellenized, the Hasmoneans, and the Hasidim. Describe each of them. Then say which were the "real Jews," and explain why that question can or cannot be answered.

3. Do an exegesis of one episode from Maccabees (1 or 2) and explain how this episode would inspire resistance to cultural compromise in ancient Judaism.

Essay Question

1. Describe the relationship of the Gentile cultures of Greece and Rome to the ethos of the New Testament community. What did they bring that helped the ancient Christian community? What did they bring that hindered it?

Quiz

1. During the intertestamental period, what conqueror seized control of the Middle East from the Persians?

a) Antiochus Epiphanes
b) Ptolemy Philadelphus
c) Jason
d) Alexander the Great

2. By the time of the New Testament, the *lingua franca* was _____.

a) Greek democracy
b) Greek religion
c) Greek language
d) Greek philosophy

3. Jews who assimilated themselves to Greek culture were called
_____.

a) Hellenizers
b) Hasideans
c) Kittim
d) Pharisees

4. What is the name of the ruler who tried to force Greek culture, including idolatry, on the Jews?

a) Pompey
b) Ptolemy Philadelphus
c) Antiochus Epiphanes
d) Cleopatra

5. Resistance against the attempt to force Greek culture on the Jews was led by a family known as the _____.

a) Maccabees
b) Sadducees
c) Pharisees
d) Ptolemies

6. What Roman general seized control of Palestine from the family who had led a revolt against the forcing of Greek culture on Palestinian Jews?

a) Julius Caesar
b) Pompey

c) Mark Antony
d) Octavian

7. The spread of Christianity was facilitated by the _____.

   a) Pax Romana
   b) Jewish revolts in the first and second centuries AD
   c) Misrule of Archelaus
   d) Roman governors over Judea

8. Jesus was born under the emperorship of _____.

   a) Augustus
   b) Nero
   c) Claudius
   d) Tiberius

9. Jesus ministered in public and died during the emperorship of
_____.

   a) Augustus
   b) Domitian
   c) Claudius
   d) Tiberius

10. During what year were Jerusalem and the temple destroyed in
the Romans' crushing of a major Jewish revolt?

   a) 4 BC
   b) AD 33
   c) AD 70
   d) AD 135

CHAPTER 2

The Mundane Settings of the New Testament

You Should Know

- Jewish and Gentile populations were thoroughly mixed at the time of the New Testament.

- Palestine was not as technologically developed nor as socially stratified as the more Gentile cities in the Roman Empire.

- The Roman Empire's knack for infrastructure and order aided the spread of the gospel.

- Roman civilization was more liberal with sex and violence than Jewish society.

- Because a person's personality was dyadic, or determined by how others perceived him, shame and honor were the most important values for society.

- Ancient people were surprisingly advanced in engineering, science, and medicine, even in light of contemporary standards.

- Honor and shame: consisted in public recognition of one's status in society, whatever that status was; consisted in concern for one's honor

- The family: the basic unit of society

- Social classes: classes were sharply stratified in pagan society

- Entertainment: reflected the immorality of society and fed on bloodlust in the gladiatorial games

Reflection Questions

1. How might the media and transportation of messages in the ancient world contribute to their content or significance? How does that differ in regard to the speed and convenience of our own forms of media today?

2. Ancient culture was thoroughly hierarchical, even within the context of the family. What were the advantages and disadvantages of ancient familial hierarchy and roles?

3. How does the Greco-Roman understanding of entertainment reflect society today? How might Christianity respond?

Essay Question

1. Who were the most hated people in the ancient Jewish world, and why? Who might be the most hated person in our own society? What would Christianity do with a person like that?

Quiz

1. In the first century:
   a) More Jews lived in Palestine than elsewhere in the Roman Empire
   b) Fewer Jews lived in Palestine than elsewhere in the Roman Empire
   c) More Jews lived outside the Roman Empire than in the Roman Empire
   d) None of the above

2. The legal language of the Roman Empire was _____.
   a) Greek
   b) Aramaic
   c) Hebrew
   d) None of the above

3. What city had a library of well over half a million volumes?

   a) Alexandria
   b) Antioch
   c) Athens
   d) Rome

4. The average daily diet in the Roman Empire included _____.

   a) Red meat
   b) Fruit and vegetables
   c) Seafood
   d) All of the above

5. First-century Roman society featured _____.

   a) A strong middle class
   b) Few slaves
   c) Homeless, foodless mobs
   d) None of the above

6. In Palestine, a majority of the population lived _____.

   a) In large cities, such as Jerusalem
   b) In rural villages
   c) On farms in the countryside
   d) In man-made caves

7. Slavery in the Roman Empire:

   a) Was racially based (as in pre–Civil War America)
   b) Included only those of no education
   c) Did not exist in Jewish society or Christian households
   d) Provided a means of at least temporary economic security for those who sold themselves into slavery

8. Crucifixion was imposed on:

   a) Slaves who had turned criminal
   b) Free people convicted of heinous crimes
   c) Jewish rebels against Rome
   d) All of the above

9. A dyadic personality is determined largely by:
    a) One's own, independently established self-image
    b) Others' attribution of honor or shame
    c) Psychological neuroses
    d) None of the above

10. In the Roman Empire the practice of medicine:
    a) Lacked surgical techniques and instruments
    b) Made extensive use of anesthetics
    c) Included the filling of teeth and the use of false teeth
    d) None of the above

CHAPTER 3

The Religious and Philosophical Settings of the New Testament

You Should Know

- The moral monotheism of Judaism stood in stark contrast to the liberal polytheism of the Greeks and Romans in antiquity.

- Most people in antiquity were superstitious syncretists who borrowed from different religions and philosophical schools.

- Many Gentiles were attracted to the ethics and the robust monotheism of Judaism.

- Judaism broke into several factions disagreeing about culture (Hebraists and Hellenists), religion (Pharisees, Sadducees, Essenes), and politics (Herodians and Zealots).

- The Jewish worship of the temple and synagogue, as well as the Jewish Scriptures, was the basis of Christianity, which would also integrate the intelligence of its Gentile converts.

- Christianity emerged at a time when both Gentile society and Jewish society were divided and confused, and it often found itself at odds with both.

- Emperor worship: the practice of deifying Augustus and subsequent emperors who had served well

- Mystery religions: the cults of Eleusis, Mithra, Isis, Dionysus, Cybele, and many local cults

- Gnosticism: took shape in the first century and equated matter with evil, spirit with good

- Dead Sea Scrolls: approximately eight hundred scrolls discovered in caves near the ruins of Qumran just off the northwest shore of the Dead Sea, containing literature similar to the traditional pseudepigrapha

Reflection Questions

1. Jesus often traveled to Jerusalem for Jewish festivals, and the New Testament records important events in his life related to certain festivals. What are they and how do they amplify the significance of his actions?

2. How are elements of the temple and the synagogue present in Christian worship? What Christian denominations emphasize one more than another? What is the emphasis in your own community's worship?

3. How would early Christian worship appeal to adherents to mystery religions such as Mithras, Isis, and Dionysius? How did the early Christians distance themselves from the unsavory elements of these mystery cults?

Essay Question

1. Which elements of ancient Greek philosophy have made it into Christian practice and which elements have not?

Quiz

1. The Greek, or pagan, hierarchy of gods is known as the _____.
    a) Pantheon
    b) Pontifex maximus
    c) Shema
    d) Augury

2. Roman emperors were:
   a) Deified after their deaths by the Roman senate if they had ruled well
   b) Refused deification by the Roman senate if they had deified themselves before dying
   c) Deified by people in eastern Roman provinces prior to the emperors' deaths
   d) All of the above

3. Mystery religions promised _____.
   a) Purification
   b) Immortality
   c) Both of the above
   d) Neither of the above

4. The term "Gnosticism" comes from the Greek word for _____.
   a) Asceticism
   b) Libertinism
   c) Immortality
   d) Knowledge

5. The Jewish religious sect consisting of high-ranking priests and aristocratic laymen was the _____.
   a) Essenes
   b) Zealots
   c) Sadducees
   d) Pharisees

6. After the crushing of Jewish revolts against Rome, Judaism became:
   a) More dominated by Pharisaic tradition
   b) Less legalistic
   c) Both of the above
   d) Neither of the above

7. Which was the center of Jewish worship during religious festivals?
   a) The home
   b) The synagogue

   c) The temple
   d) None of the above

8. The Dead Sea Scrolls were found mainly in caves near _____.
   a) Qumran
   b) Chenoboskion
   c) Nag Hammadi
   d) A & C

9. Jewish religious festivals to which pilgrims thronged were _____.
   a) Passover-Unleavened Bread, Pentecost, and Tabernacles
   b) Pentecost and Trumpets/Rosh Hashanah
   c) Yom Kipper and Hanukkah
   d) Purim, Lights, and Trumpets

10. First-century Jews expected their Messiah to:
   a) Suffer and die for their sins
   b) Be divine as well as human
   c) Rule with kingly power
   d) None of the above

CHAPTER 4

The Canon of the New Testament

You Should Know

- The canon is the "measuring reed" or standard of books which the early church considered to be divinely inspired.

- *Homolegoumena* are books that were quickly confessed by all to be divinely inspired.

- *Antilegoumena* were books whose authorship was not immediately obvious.

- The chief criterion was apostolicity or authorship by an apostle.

- The integration and citation of NT books by the early church fathers helped establish canonicity.

- Codices of papyrus were the primary format for NT books.

- There are many modern translations in English aided by the recent discoveries of many papyri fragments over the past 150 years.

- Canon: the books accepted by the church as the standard that governs Christian beliefs and conduct

- Apostolicity: the criteria for canonicity of a book being written by an apostle or apostolic associate

- Textual criticism: The exercise of determining the original wording of the New Testament

Reflection Questions

1. What was the role of the church fathers and Marcion in the development of the NT canon?

2. What is the basis of NT canonicity and why were some books excluded?

3. Given the substantial differences in the New Testament manuscripts that we have, how can a modern reader have confidence that they are reading God's Word?

Essay Question

1. Describe the four main rules for evaluation in textual criticism.

Quiz

1. Early Christians:
    a) Accepted the Old Testament as divinely inspired Scripture
    b) Refused to accept the Old Testament as divinely inspired Scripture
    c) Differed widely among themselves on whether to accept the Old Testament as divinely inspired Scripture
    d) None of the above

2. Apostolicity means _____.
    a) Authorship by an apostle
    b) Authorship by a close associate of an apostle
    c) Both of the above
    d) Neither of the above

3. The term "canon" developed the metaphorical meaning _____.
    a) Knowledge
    b) Standard
    c) Together
    d) All of the above

4. The New Testament canon consists of the _____.
    a) Subapostolic writings
    b) New Testament apocrypha

c) Oxyrhynchus papyri
d) None of the above

5. In the second century, Marcion drew up a New Testament canon which by comparison with ours is _____.

   a) The same
   b) Longer
   c) Shorter
   d) None of the above

6. Influencing Marcion's choices for the New Testament canon was his:

   a) Anti-Judaism
   b) Pro-Judaism
   c) Anti-Gnosticism
   d) B & C

7. The earliest Christian writings that have survived besides the books of the New Testament were written by the _____.

   a) Gnostics
   b) Apostles
   c) Apostolic fathers
   d) Churches

8. The writing secretary for an ancient author is known by the term _____.

   a) Lectionary
   b) *Amanuensis*
   c) Teacher
   d) *Apostolos*

9. In relation to the New Testament, textual criticism means determining its _____.

   a) Original wording
   b) Historical accuracy
   c) Theological accuracy
   d) All of the above

10. Chapter and verse divisions in the Bible:

a) Appeared in the first-century originals
b) Originated in second-century copies
c) Originated in the late Middle Ages
d) Originated in the modern period

CHAPTER 5

The Story of Jesus's Life

You Should Know

- There are historical references to Christ, attributed but unwritten sayings of Christ, collected sayings of Christ, and apocryphal gospels.

- Higher criticism tries to answer questions about authorship, audience, and the relation of the Gospels to one another.

- Markan priority is the most popular and likely understanding of the Gospels' relations to one another.

- There are many forms of higher criticism that yield different readings of Jesus's life.

- There was a considerable push in the modern period to discover the life of the historical Jesus and discover his authentic sayings.

- Apocryphal gospels: postapostolic writings presenting a motley mixture of heretical beliefs and pious imaginations filling out the details of Jesus's life and teachings

- Synoptic problem: why the first three Gospels are very much alike

- Marcan priority: hypothesis that Matthew and Luke based most of their narrative on Mark, drawing most of Jesus's sayings and teachings from a lost document known as Q

- Higher criticism: determining the historical circumstances of the New Testament books

- Form criticism: determining oral tradition prior to writing

Reflection Questions

1. Define and describe form criticism. What are the major problems with this method and how has it impacted gospel studies?

2. Describe the arguments in favor and against the existence of Q. What arguments do you find compelling and why?

3. Identify and describe the major scholarly movements that have sought to reconstruct the life of the "historical Jesus."

Essay Question

1. Define the synoptic problem, the two-source hypothesis, the two-gospel hypothesis, and the Augustinian theory. Provide two strengths and two weaknesses of each solution to the synoptic problem.

Quiz

1. The mention of Jesus by several ancient secular historians _____.
   a) Provides little information about Jesus for the reconstruction of his career
   b) Disproves the view that Jesus was purely legendary
   c) Both of the above
   d) Neither of the above

2. The Gospel of Thomas:
   a) Was written by the apostle Thomas
   b) Is a narrative of Jesus's life
   c) Is still disputed by scholars today
   d) None of the above

3. The church father who gives the earliest information about the writing of the canonical Gospels, their authorship, etc. is _____.
   a) Papias
   b) Marcion

    c) Pliny the Younger

    d) Augustine

4. The Synoptic Gospels include:

    a) Matthew, Mark, and Luke

    b) Luke and John

    c) Mark, Luke, and John

    d) Matthew, Mark, and John

5. The title of Albert Schweitzer's survey of modern studies of Jesus's life is _____.

    a) *The Quest of the Historical Jesus*

    b) *The History of the Synoptic Tradition*

    c) *The Apostolic Preaching and Its Development*

    d) *The Life and Times of Jesus the Messiah*

6. Form criticism deals with:

    a) The basic evangelistic message of early Christians

    b) The synoptic problem

    c) The overall theological editorship on the part of the gospel writers

    d) Development of tradition about Jesus through oral stages to canonical writings

7. Source criticism deals with:

    a) The basic evangelistic message of early Christians

    b) The synoptic problem

    c) The overall theological editorship on the part of the Gospel writers

    d) Development of tradition about Jesus through oral stages to canonical writings

8. Concerning the Gospels, conservative scholars accept:

    a) Topical as well as chronological arrangements

    b) Paraphrase as well as direct quotation of Jesus's words

    c) The trustworthiness of the contents

    d) All of the above

9. By definition, the term *"kerygma"* means _____.
   a) Proclamation
   b) Immediately
   c) Good news
   d) Teaching

10. What tries to establish the story line of a gospel?
    a) Narrative criticism
    b) Tradition criticism
    c) Rhetorical criticism
    d) Canon criticism

CHAPTER 6

An Introductory Overview of Jesus's Public Life and Ministry

You Should Know

- Jesus's ministry is divided into a year of obscurity, a year of popularity, and a year of rejection.

- Most of Jesus's ministry took place in Galilee, particularly in Capernaum.

- Jesus had his close group of twelve apostles and an ever-increasing crowd following him.

- His teaching was based on ethical monotheism of Judaism and was often expressed through parables.

- His major theme, the kingdom of God (or "heaven"), is often understood either as a realized eschatology or a consistent eschatology.

- An example of "kingdom" as the activity of ruling: "The kingdom of God is in your midst [or 'within'] you" (Luke 17:21). In other words, "God reigns 'amidst' [or within] you."

- An example of "kingdom" as the sphere of rule: "How hard it is for the rich to enter the kingdom of God!" (Luke 18:24). In other words, "How hard it is for the rich to enter the sphere where God rules!"

- John the Baptist: a hermit-like prophet who preached to crowds and baptized people in preparation for the coming of God's kingdom

- Parable: extended figures of speech in story form

- Son of Man: Daniel's vision of a superhuman figure coming from heaven to judge and rule the whole world

Reflection Questions

1. What aspects of Jesus's life and teaching do modern people tend to find unacceptable—intellectually, aesthetically, and socially—in comparison with ancient people? Why?

2. Explain the difference, if any, between "the kingdom of God" and "the kingdom of heaven."

3. What are the two meanings of "kingdom"?

Essay Question

1. Explain the difference between realized eschatology and consistent eschatology, and the "mystery" of the kingdom (or inaugurated eschatology).

Quiz

1. Traditionally, Jesus's public ministry has been divided into periods of _____.
    a) Obscurity and popularity
    b) Popularity and rejection
    c) Obscurity, popularity, and rejection
    d) Popularity, rejection, and revival

2. Jesus's public ministry is usually calculated to have lasted how many years?
    a) One and a half
    b) Two and a half
    c) Three and a half
    d) Five

3. Jesus's temptation by Satan _____.

    a) Preceded Jesus's baptism

    b) Occurred during Jesus's baptism

    c) Followed Jesus's baptism

    d) Followed Jesus's calling of his first disciples

4. When confessed as the Messiah, Jesus started predicting his _____.

    a) Transfiguration

    b) Death and resurrection

    c) Ascension to heaven

    d) Second coming

5. The Last Supper was a _____.

    a) Passover meal

    b) Love feast

    c) Sermon

    d) Prayer

6. The crucifixion of Jesus lasted:

    a) From early morning till noon

    b) From midmorning till midafternoon

    c) From noon till late afternoon

    d) From late afternoon through early evening

7. Jesus's resurrection happened:

    a) Very early Sunday morning

    b) Midmorning on Sunday

    c) Noon on Sunday

    d) Sunday afternoon

8. Supporting the reality of Jesus's miracles is:

    a) Other religions never laying claim to the miraculous

    b) Early Christians' tenacity in maintaining their testimony under the pressure of persecution

    c) Both of the above

    d) Neither of the above

9. Jesus's parables:
    a) Never contain more than one point
    b) Sometimes contain more than one point
    c) Always contain more than one point
    d) None of the above

10. The term "kingdom" means _____.
    a) The activity of ruling
    b) The sphere of rule
    c) Both of the above
    d) Neither of the above

CHAPTER 7

Mark

An Apology for the Crucifixion of Jesus

You Should Know

- According to tradition, the Gospel of Mark was probably written in Rome in the late fifties or early sixties by John Mark, who was dependent upon the apostle Peter.

- Mark's Gospel is a fast-paced dramatic portrayal of Jesus's ministry.

- Mark likely wrote this Gospel to inspire and convert new Christians by counteracting the shame of Jesus's crucifixion.

- Mark likely wrote for a Gentile and, more specifically, Roman audience.

- The material found in Mark 16:9–20 is most likely a later addition to the narrative, not part of Mark's original Gospel.

- Gospels: books that deal with the life and ministry of Jesus

- Evangelist: the author of a Gospel, meaning "proclaimer of good news"

- Christ: means "anointed" in the sense of one chosen by God for a special task, in the bringing of God's kingdom

- Olivet Discourse: Jesus's ability to predict the fates of the temple, of the world, and of the elect and of his own return at the end of history as presently known

- Mark's ending: The best textual tradition stops with Mark 16:8. Inferior traditions add 16:9–20, called the long ending, and a shorter, unnumbered ending, both generally recognized as inauthentic.

Reflection Questions

1. Identify and evaluate the suggested purposes of Mark's writing.

2. What can we know about Mark's audience? Are they "insiders," "outsiders," or both, but affected in different ways?

3. What question plagues the ending of Mark?

Essay Question

1. With regard to the "messianic secret," choose several passages where Jesus commands his disciples to be silent about his messianic identity or works, and explain what his reason for this is.

Quiz

1. A tradition dating from early in the second century states that the Gospel of Mark contains the reminiscences of what apostle concerning Jesus?

    a) Peter
    b) James
    c) John
    d) Thomas

2. Overall, Mark portrays Jesus as the _____.

    a) Mighty and authoritative Son of God
    b) Meek and mild Messiah
    c) Ideal human being
    d) None of the above

3. The "messianic secret" in Mark refers to _____.

a) Jesus's suppression of publicity concerning his messiahship
b) The failure of most Jews to recognize Jesus as the Messiah
c) Both of the above
d) Neither of the above

4. Mark uses a number of terms in what language besides Greek?

a) Hebrew
b) Aramaic
c) Syriac
d) Latin

5. Mark's version of Jesus's temptation emphasizes the acknowledgment of Jesus's status as God's Son by _____.

a) Satan
b) Wild beasts
c) Angels
d) All of the above

6. Which of the following statements is NOT true?

a) In Mark, Jesus exercises authority to forgive sins
b) In Mark, Jesus eats with tax collectors and sinners
c) In Mark, Jesus defends his disciples' practice of fasting
d) In Mark, Jesus lets his disciples pluck grain on the Sabbath

7. In Mark, Jesus speaks in parables to:

a) Obscure the truth judgmentally from outsiders
b) Clarify the truth with interpretation for insiders
c) Both of the above
d) Neither of the above

8. In Mark, when Peter says Jesus is the Christ, Jesus:

a) Rebukes Peter for saying so
b) Commends Peter for saying so
c) Tells Peter and the other disciples to spread the news that he is the Christ
d) None of the above

9. Jesus compared his upcoming suffering and death to:

   a) Drinking from a cup
   b) Being baptized
   c) A trial
   d) A & B

10. Mark counteracts the shame of Jesus's crucifixion by noting that:

   a) Jesus did not have to carry his own cross
   b) Jesus was offered wine mixed with myrrh
   c) Jesus hung on the cross only six hours
   d) All of the above

CHAPTER 8

Matthew

Handbook for a Mixed Church under Persecution

You Should Know

- Matthew was most likely written by the apostle Matthew before AD 70 in Antioch, Syria, for a primarily Jewish audience.

- The Gospel was written to strengthen Jewish Christians in their suffering of persecution, to warn them against laxity and apostasy, and to urge them to use their persecution as an opportunity for the evangelism of all nations.

- This Gospel lends prominence to five teaching sections of Jesus that recalls Moses's encounter with God on Mount Sinai.

- Matthew, perhaps more than any other Gospel writer, asserts that Jesus's life and teaching are a fulfillment of OT prophecy.

- Jesus proclaims a kingdom that runs contrary to Jewish expectations, especially as he ends by commissioning his apostles to go out to all nations.

- Matthew's account of Jesus's crucifixion highlights the indignities done to Jesus as a victim of persecution and his kingship and divine sonship.

- Typology: historical events, persons, and institutions divinely intended to be prefigurative, quite apart from whether or not the authors of the Old Testament were aware of the predictive symbolism

- Sermon on the Mount: Jesus ascends a mountain, takes the seated position of a teacher, and teaches his disciples.

- Transfiguration: an experience on a mountain in which Peter, James, and John gain understanding of Jesus as the new and greater Moses, where Jesus's face shines as that of Moses in consequence of his meeting with God on Mount Sinai

- Great Commission: Jesus told his disciples to make disciples of all nations, baptize converts, and teach converts to keep all his commandments.

Reflection Questions

1. In and for which region did Matthew write his Gospel? How did that characterize the message found in his Gospel?

2. Describe the purpose of the Gospel of Matthew with reference to its major themes (with scriptural support).

3. Matthew alternates between narrative and discourse in five major sections—Sermon on the Mount, the Missionary Discourse, the Parables of the Kingdom, the Church and the Kingdom, and the Judgment Discourse. How do the narrative elements complement the teaching they surround?

Essay Question

1. What are some unique contributions to our understanding of Jesus given by Matthew? Choose several Jewish laws or customs that Jesus rewrites in the course of his ministry and explain why his authority was challenging to his contemporaries.

Quiz

1. The apostle Matthew appears in other Gospels under the name _____.

a) Thaddeus
b) Levi
c) Bartholomew
d) Zebedee

2. How does Matthew usually treat Mark's narrative?

a) He lengthens it
b) He maintains its length
c) He condenses it
d) He omits it

3. The number of Jesus's long discourses in Matthew contributes to a portrayal of Jesus as a new and greater _____.

a) Moses
b) Joshua
c) Elijah
d) David

4. Matthew's genealogy of Jesus:

a) Omits several generations known from the Old Testament
b) Can be related to the numerical value of David's name in Hebrew
c) Includes several Gentile women
d) All of the above

5. The flight of the holy family to Egypt and their return fulfilled Hosea 11:1, which originally referred to:

a) Abraham going to and from Egypt
b) The exodus of Israel from Egypt
c) The flight of some Jews to Egypt at the time of Jeremiah
d) The flight of Jeroboam to Egypt

6. In Matthew, "This is my beloved Son, in whom I am well pleased," shows that:

a) God took pleasure in Jesus's insistence on getting baptized
b) John the Baptist was correct in trying not to baptize Jesus
c) God saves through works done by his followers
d) Jesus was adopted at his baptism

7. Which disciples of Jesus saw him transfigured?

   a) Peter, James, and John
   b) Peter and James
   c) James and John
   d) Peter and John

8. In Matthew, Jesus emphasizes the _____.

   a) Secrecy of his second coming
   b) Visibility of his second coming
   c) Delay in his second coming
   d) None of the above

9. At the death of Jesus, who confessed his divine sonship?

   a) Peter, standing at a distance
   b) Women disciples, standing at a distance
   c) A few of the Sanhedrin
   d) A centurion and his fellow soldiers

10. In the Great Commission, Jesus told his disciples to:

   a) Make disciples of all nations
   b) Baptize converts
   c) Teach converts to keep all his commandments
   d) All of the above

CHAPTER 9

Luke

A Promotion of Christianity in the Greco-Roman World

You Should Know

- The author of Luke-Acts traveled with Paul on several occasions and is probably the only Gentile author in the NT.

- Luke is the longest book in the NT and his authorship of Acts makes Luke the most prolific author in the NT.

- Luke is the only Gospel that names its recipient (Theophilus).

- Luke traces Jesus's genealogy back to Adam, as his primary audience is Gentiles.

- The poor, the outcast, and the socially marginalized take center stage and are the recipients of salvation in Luke's Gospel.

- Luke emphasizes the universality of the gospel, prayer in the life of Jesus, and the role of the Holy Spirit.

- The Kaddish: an ancient Jewish prayer that may have provided a base for the Lord's Prayer taught by Jesus

- Trio of parables: the lost sheep, the lost coin, the prodigal son

- Via Dolorosa: the leading of Jesus away as a procession in which Simon the Cyrenian carries the cross behind Jesus and a large multitude of the people and of mourning women follow

- Emmaus disciples: The testimony of two disciples outside the circle of the Eleven that supplements that of the two angels who appeared as men at the empty tomb, arising out of a personal encounter with the risen Jesus

Reflection Questions

1. Is Luke's Gospel classless or is it suited to a particular group of people, either ancient or modern?

2. Identify ways in which the Gospel of Luke and the Book of Acts are related to one another. What difference would it make if one were to regard them as one book?

3. What in Luke's message would make him emphasize Jesus's going away in the ascension and the underemphasis on his second coming?

Essay Question

1. Explain with scriptural support the major thematic purposes of the Gospel of Luke.

Quiz

1. The author of Luke got information from _____.
    a) Eyewitnesses of Jesus's life
    b) Earlier written accounts of Jesus's life
    c) Both of the above
    d) Neither of the above

2. Luke's most distinctive contribution to our knowledge of the career of Jesus has to do with his _____.
    a) Itineration in Galilee
    b) Last journey to Jerusalem
    c) Ministry in Samaria
    d) Excursion to the Dead Sea

3. The mental, physical, spiritual, and social development of the boy Jesus portrays him primarily as a(n) _____.

    a) Normal Jewish boy

    b) Ideal human being

    c) Normal human being

    d) None of the above

4. Luke's Gospel pays special attention to _____.

    a) Social outcasts

    b) Women

    c) Both of the above

    d) Neither of the above

5. Luke's version of Jesus's temptation:

    a) Portrays Jesus as full of the Holy Spirit

    b) Portrays Jesus as being led by the Holy Spirit in the wilderness

    c) Highlights Jesus's moral victory in the devil's finishing every temptation and departing

    d) All of the above

6. In comparison with Matthew's version of the Lord's Prayer, Luke's version is _____.

    a) Longer

    b) Shorter

    c) Equal in length

    d) Interspersed with Luke's editorial comments

7. Luke's account of the preparation and eating of the Passover emphasizes:

    a) Jesus as a law-abiding Jew

    b) Table fellowship

    c) After-dinner drinking and conversation

    d) All of the above

8. As cited by Luke, Jesus's final words from the cross were which of the following?

a) "My God, my God, why have you forsaken me?"
b) "I thirst!"
c) "Father, into your hands I commit my spirit!"
d) "It is finished!"

9. After his resurrection, Jesus traveled and conversed with two of his disciples on their way to _____.

a) Bethlehem
b) Emmaus
c) Pella
d) Galilee

10. Luke ends his Gospel with an account of Jesus's:

a) Resurrection
b) Post-resurrection ministry
c) Ascension
d) Sending of the Holy Spirit

CHAPTER 10

John
Believing in Jesus for Eternal Life

You Should Know

- The Gospel of John was most likely written by the apostle John, who was the "Beloved Disciple," between the years AD 80–85.

- John's Gospel supplements the Synoptic Gospels.

- The purpose of writing is to clarify that Jesus is the Word "made flesh" (to counter the claims of the Gnostics) and believing in him grants one eternal life.

- The language of John's Gospel involves a selective and rich vocabulary, explicit declarations, symbolism, and irony.

- The book is divided into two sections—the Book of Signs and the Book of Glory.

- John's Gospel seems to correct followers of John the Baptist, Jews, and Gnostics.

- Rylands Fragment of John: This papyrus fragment dates from about AD 135 and requires several previous decades for the writing, copying, and circulation of John as far as the Egyptian hinterland, where the fragment was discovered.

- Johannine emphasis: Jesus in Judea, long discourses, eternal life

- Realized eschatology: When people believe, they receive eternal life immediately.

- The Holy Spirit as paraclete: consoles believers in Jesus's absence, teaches believers what Jesus has said and will yet say, and convicts unbelievers of their rejection of Jesus

Reflection Questions

1. Identify and explain the addressees and purpose of the Gospel of John.

2. Choose one pericope from John's Gospel and discuss how its inclusion presents a different aspect of Jesus's life when compared with the Synoptics.

3. Explain how Jesus redefined a symbol attached to each major feast or facet of Jewish life.

Essay Question

1. Describe the Christology of John's Gospel. How is Jesus presented in this Gospel?

Quiz

1. Most importantly testifying to authorship of the fourth Gospel by the apostle John is the early church father _____.
   - a) Irenaeus
   - b) Justin Martyr
   - c) Jerome
   - d) Tertullian

2. The fourth Gospel emphasizes Jesus's _____.
   - a) Words
   - b) Works
   - c) Both of the above
   - d) Neither of the above

3. Preeminently, John writes to engender _____.

    a) Repentance
    b) Belief
    c) Patience
    d) Hope

4. The fourth Gospel presents eternal life as:

    a) Not given until the age to come
    b) Inaugurated now but not fully given till the end
    c) Given fully now
    d) None of the above

5. Jesus compared his body to a _____.

    a) Temple
    b) Sacrifice
    c) Tomb
    d) None of the above

6. The story of the raising of Lazarus symbolizes:

    a) The resurrection of Jesus
    b) The resurrection of unbelievers at the Last Day
    c) The resurrection of believers at the Last Day
    d) All of the above

7. Jesus promised that the Holy Spirit would:

    a) Console believers in Jesus's absence
    b) Teach believers what Jesus has said and will yet say
    c) Convict unbelievers of the rejection of Jesus
    d) All of the above

8. Jesus portrayed his death and resurrection as:

    a) A judgment against the world
    b) The world's judgment against him
    c) A descent into hell and back
    d) None of the above

9. Before dying on a cross, Jesus committed his mother into the care of _____.

a) Peter
b) James
c) Thomas
d) None of the above

10. When seeing the risen Jesus, Mary:

a) Thinks he is the gardener
b) Thinks he has removed Jesus's body
c) Calls him "Lord"
d) All of the above

CHAPTER 11

Acts

A Promotion of Christianity in the Greco-Roman World at Large

You Should Know

- Acts serves as a bridge between the Gospels and the Epistles.

- The book follows the spread of the gospel from Jerusalem to the "ends of the earth" and it abruptly ends with Paul in Rome.

- Acts is a work of historiography, which accounts for Greco-Roman appreciation of travelogues, table fellowship, and high religious and moral conduct.

- Chapters 1–12 follow the apostle Peter and 13–28 follow the apostle Paul.

- The Jerusalem Council makes a decision that Gentile believers are not required to be circumcised and obey the Jewish food laws.

- The Tübingen Hypothesis: an outmoded notion that a second-century author wrote Acts to reconcile the supposedly conflicting standpoints of Petrine and Pauline Christianity

- Day of Pentecost: brings the promised baptism in the Spirit, accompanied by wind and tongue-shaped flames of fire

- Judaizers: Jewish believers who taught that Gentile believers must submit to circumcision, as prescribed by Moses, or they cannot be saved

- The Way: the first name used for Christianity

- "Christians": Disciples were called "Christians" first in Antioch, though originally the designation may have carried a derisive connotation.

Reflection Questions

1. Recount the proceedings of the Jerusalem Council and explain what we learn about the balance of authority between the early apostles.

2. Luke writes, "The disciples were called Christians first in Antioch" (Acts 11:26). What does this mean for the forming of early Christian identity? What does it mean regarding relations with Jerusalem?

3. Is Acts a biography or a history?

Essay Question

1. Discuss three ways in which Acts can contribute to the edification of believers.

Quiz

1. The main purpose of Acts was to:
    a) Show that Christianity deserved continued freedom because it was not politically disloyal to Rome
    b) Give a comprehensive survey of early church history
    c) Give a biography of the apostle Paul
    d) Trace the triumphant progress of the gospel from Jerusalem to Rome

2. When did Jesus's disciples receive the Holy Spirit?
    a) At the Festival of Purim
    b) On the Day of Pentecost
    c) On Yom Kippur
    d) After Jesus's death

3. Who is the most prominent figure in Acts 1–12?

   a) Paul
   b) Barnabas
   c) James
   d) Peter

4. Who is the most prominent figure in Acts 13–28?

   a) Paul
   b) Barnabas
   c) James
   d) Peter

5. In Acts, who first preached the gospel to a group of Gentiles?

   a) Philip
   b) Stephen
   c) Peter
   d) Paul

6. The chairman of the Jerusalem Council, who made the suggestion which the Council adopted, was _____.

   a) Titus
   b) Silas
   c) James
   d) Apollos

7. In what city did Paul spend as much as two years in prison under those governors?

   a) Joppa
   b) Caesarea
   c) Lydda
   d) Azotus

8. Where was Paul imprisoned?

   a) Philippi
   b) Caesarea
   c) Rome
   d) All of the above

9. Paul had his greatest evangelistic success with _____.

   a) Jews
   b) Gentile proselytes and God-fearers
   c) Pagan Gentiles
   d) Roman officials

10. Who preached in Ephesus prior to Paul but was ignorant of baptism in Jesus's name?

   a) Apollos
   b) Barnabas
   c) Philip's daughters
   d) Claudius

CHAPTER 12

The Early Letters of Paul

You Should Know

- Paul invented a new literary genre with his letters due to their length and depth.

- Literary differences between Paul's letters can be attributed to amanuenses.

- Paul's letters appear in the NT according to descending length.

- The Galatians are primarily Gentiles who are pressured by Judaizers to come under the Mosaic law and receive circumcision.

- Both 1 and 2 Thessalonians were written from Corinth on Paul's second missionary journey.

- In 1 Thessalonians, Paul congratulates and comforts believers who have suffered the death of several believers in their community.

- In 2 Thessalonians, Paul corrects a fanatic eschatology that arose in the church apparently inspired by a longing to be delivered from persecution.

- *Amanuensis*: professional scribe

- *Parenesis*: a closing section containing ethical instructions

- Justify: God's treating believers in Christ as just—that is, righteous—even though they are sinners

Reflection Questions

1. What was the original intent of circumcision and why does Paul not encourage it among the Galatians?

2. Explain the nature of Peter and Paul's argument in Galatians 2:11–14 and how that helps us date the letter with regard to Acts.

3. Is Paul's imperative to "pray continually" (1 Thessalonians 5:17) related to the eschatology(ies) found in these letters? Why or why not?

Essay Question

1. Compare and contrast the theme of eschatology in 1 and 2 Thessalonians.

Quiz

1. The first major section of Galatians is:
   a) A discussion of the rejection of Israel
   b) An autobiographical argument for divine grace against law-righteousness
   c) A theological argument for divine grace against law-righteousness
   d) A warning against the attitude that divine grace gives license to sin

2. What is the third major section of Galatians?
   a) A discussion of the rejection of Israel
   b) An autobiographical argument for divine grace against law-righteousness
   c) A theological argument for divine grace against law-righteousness
   d) A warning against the attitude that divine grace gives license to sin

3. Paul's greatest example of justification in the Old Testament is _____.

   a) Isaiah
   b) Job

    c) Moses

    d) Abraham

4. "Antinomianism" means _____.

    a) Making someone righteous

    b) Regarding someone as righteous

    c) Taking license to sin because of divine grace

    d) Satisfaction of God's wrath against sinners by means of a sub-stitutionary sacrifice

5. In Galatians, works contrast with _____.

    a) Faith

    b) Promise

    c) Law

    d) Spirit

6. The content of 1 Thessalonians generally has to do with which of the following?

    a) Congratulations on Christian progress and exhortations, especially concerning the second coming

    b) False teaching of a proto-Gnostic variety

    c) The Old Testament law and justification

    d) None of the above

7. (T/F) The Christian virtue "hope" means confident expectation of Jesus's second coming.

8. According to Paul, the Day of the Lord will come unexpectedly on _____.

    a) Christians

    b) Non-Christians

    c) All human beings

    d) The demonic world

9. What is the second major section of Galatians?

    a) A discussion of the rejection of Israel

    b) An autobiographical argument for divine grace against law-righteousness

c) A theological argument for divine grace against law-righteousness

d) A warning against the attitude that divine grace gives license to sin

10. According to 2 Thessalonians:

a) Christians in Thessalonica had come to believe that Jesus's second coming lay in the distant future

b) Paul urged the Christians in Thessalonica to prepare for a possible immediate return of Jesus

c) Both of the above

d) Neither of the above

CHAPTER 13

The Major Letters of Paul

You Should Know

- Paul wrote at least two other letters to the Corinthians that we do not have.

- Corinth was a cosmopolitan city known for sexual immorality and the Corinthians tended to be very concerned with outward appearances and social standing.

- Paul wrote 1 Corinthians in Ephesus on his third missionary journey and 2 Corinthians was written after Paul had made a "painful" visit.

- A divisive group of "super-apostles" began breaking apart the Corinthian community and disparaged Paul by accusing him of a weak appearance and unsophisticated speech.

- Romans is an uncontested writing of Paul, written in the mid-50s.

- Romans was written to both Jewish and Gentile Christians in Rome.

- The sacrificial death and resurrection of Christ is the basis for justification.

- One of Paul's purposes in writing Romans is to support his mission to Spain.

- Speaking in tongues: miraculous speaking of unlearned human languages

- Process of salvation according to Romans 8:30: predestined, called, justified, glorified

Reflection Questions

1. Explain Paul's understanding of the role played in the church by the gift of tongues. What is its use? What is the standard by which it is judged?

2. How is Romans a Gentile letter? How is it a Jewish letter?

3. Why shouldn't we sin, if grace abounds all the more whenever we do?

Essay Question

1. Identify and discuss three major arguments that Paul makes about the resurrection in 1 Corinthians 15.

Quiz

1. Apparently, a delegation from the Corinthian church brought to Paul which of the following?
    a) A monetary gift for the church in Jerusalem
    b) A letter asking Paul's judgment on various problems
    c) Paul's presence and help for the church
    d) All of the above

2. On the question of divorce, Paul:
    a) Repeats Jesus's teaching against divorce
    b) Tells Christians to divorce their non-Christian spouses
    c) Tells Christians with non-Christian spouses that their children are unconsecrated
    d) None of the above

3. For celebration of the Lord's Supper, Paul commands:
    a) Delay till the arrival of latecomers
    b) Continuance of associated love feasts
    c) Communal sacrifice and devotion
    d) None of the above

4. What Christian virtue does Paul rank higher than any spiritual gift?

   a) Humility
   b) Faith
   c) Patience
   d) Love

5. Some Christians in Corinth seem to have denied the _____.

   a) Resurrection of Christ in the past
   b) Resurrection of Christians in the future
   c) Both of the above
   d) Neither of the above

6. In 2 Corinthians 1–7, Paul does which of the following?

   a) Expresses relief and joy at the favorable response of most of the Corinthians
   b) Discusses food dedicated to idols
   c) Defends his apostolic authority to a still-rebellious minority
   d) Stresses a collection for Jerusalem

7. In 2 Corinthians 10–11, Paul does which of the following?

   a) Expresses relief and joy at the favorable response of most of the Corinthians
   b) Discusses food dedicated to idols
   c) Defends his apostolic authority to a still-rebellious minority
   d) Stresses a collection for Jerusalem

8. After an introductory section containing greetings and brief descriptions of his plans, the next section of Romans deals with _____.

   a) Paul's detailed plans and a long list of personal greetings
   b) The problem of Israel's unbelief
   c) The sinfulness of humanity
   d) Justification

9. Romans 12–14 deals with _____.

   a) Practical exhortations
   b) Paul's detailed plans and a long list of personal greetings

c) Justification
d) The problem of Israel's unbelief

10. According to Paul in Romans, baptism represents _____.
   a) Repentance from sin
   b) Cleansing from sin
   c) Allegiance to Christ
   d) Union with Christ in his death, burial, and resurrection

CHAPTER 14

The Prison Letters of Paul

You Should Know

- Paul's two known imprisonments were in Caesarea under Felix and Festus and in Rome awaiting trial before Caesar. Some scholars suggest an Ephesian imprisonment as well.

- Paul asks a Christian slave master named Philemon to receive kindly, perhaps even to release, his recently converted runaway slave Onesimus, now returning.

- In Colossians, Paul combats a heresy with a correct Christology and draws out the practical implications of this high Christology for everyday life and conduct.

- Ephesians emphasizes the church as Christ's body, whereas Colossians emphasizes the headship of Christ.

- Ephesians was probably intended to be a general letter that circulated to several churches in Asia Minor.

- Paul thanks the Philippians for their financial gift, counteracts a tendency toward divisiveness in their church, warns against Judaizers, and prepares them for visits.

- Prison letters: Ephesians, Philippians, Colossians, and Philemon

- Colossians heresy: false teaching that diminished the person of Christ, emphasized human philosophy, contained elements of Judaism, included angel worship, flaunted air of secrecy and superiority

- Divine grace: Paul's teaching that salvation is wholly unearned; it comes by God's grace, through faith, and apart from meritorious good works

- Kenosis: Jesus's self-emptying, or humiliation, and exaltation through the incarnation

Reflection Questions

1. How can Paul's Christology in Colossians correct errors present in our culture and even churches today?

2. Choose one pair of relationships discussed by Paul in Ephesians (husbands, wives, children, slaves, masters, etc.) and explain how these are based on mutuality and also the work of Christ.

3. What was the key to Paul's joy in hardship, as expressed in Philippians?

Essay Question

1. Should Paul and the early Christians have crusaded against slavery? Why did they not? What should the church's involvement with social structures be in light of Philemon and the rest of the NT?

Quiz

1. The two known, extended imprisonments of Paul were in
   _____.
   a) Caesarea and Rome
   b) Philippi and Berea
   c) Ephesus and Troas
   d) Miletus and Lystra

2. Which of the following was probably a circular letter?
   a) Ephesians
   b) Philemon

c) Colossians

d) Philippians

3. The name of a slave owner in Colossae was _____.

   a) Epaphroditus

   b) Philemon

   c) Onesimus

   d) Silvanus

4. The name of a runaway slave was _____.

   a) Epaphroditus

   b) Philemon

   c) Onesimus

   d) Silvanus

5. Paul's letter called "Colossians" emphasizes what doctrine?

   a) Christology

   b) Justification

   c) The church as Christ's body

   d) Eschatology

6. Paul's letter called "Ephesians" emphasizes _____.

   a) Christology

   b) Justification

   c) The church as Christ's body

   d) Eschatology

7. What is the dominant emotional note in Paul's letter to the Philippians?

   a) Joy

   b) Sadness

   c) Discouragement

   d) None of the above

8. The so-called Colossian heresy:

   a) Diminished the person of Christ

   b) Emphasized human philosophy

c) Contained elements of Judaism and oriental mysticism
d) All of the above

9. In addition to thanking the Philippians for their financial gift in his letter to them, Paul deals with:

a) A tendency toward divisiveness in their church
b) A danger posed by Judaizers
c) His own autobiography
d) All of the above

10. The Greek word *kenosis* means:

a) Dog
b) Mutilation
c) Unity
d) None of the above

CHAPTER 15

The Pastoral Letters of Paul

You Should Know

- The Pastorals give us a great deal of insight into what qualifies a person for ministry.

- First and Second Timothy and Titus constitute the Pastoral Letters, so called because Paul writes them to young pastors (literally, "shepherds").

- The Pastorals contain instructions concerning the administrative responsibilities of Timothy and Titus in churches, plus warnings against heresy and personal matters.

- Many modern scholars claim they are pseudonymous, but Pauline authorship can be maintained because of amanuenses, development of his thought, and audience.

- First Timothy and Titus were written by Paul in Rome after he was acquitted and released from his first Roman imprisonment, and 2 Timothy was written during his second.

- In these three letters, similar problems arise in each of them, such as certain "teachers of the law" who have led the churches astray through their "myths" and debates.

- Pastoral Letters: 1 and 2 Timothy, Titus

- Gnosticism: a philosophy that borrowed its cosmological myth from Judaism, but was opposed to the other features

- Church government: elders/bishops and deacons

- Orthodoxy: completed Christian doctrine to be defended from corruption rather than widened in scope

Reflection Questions

1. What were the early church's standards regarding apostolic scriptural texts that suggest that pseudepigraphy/pseudonymity are not valid critiques of Pauline authority?

2. Why does Paul circumcise Timothy, but insists that Titus should not be circumcised?

3. What is the role of the *episkopos*, *presbyteros*, and *diakonia* in the Pastoral Epistles?

Essay Question

1. Identify and discuss the major Christological elements contained in the Pastoral Epistles.

Quiz

1. The tradition that Paul himself wrote the Pastoral Letters is

_____.

   a) Late
   b) Weak
   c) Disputed
   d) None of the above

2. "Orthodoxy" means:
   a) Right belief
   b) Right conduct
   c) Right friendships
   d) All of the above

3. "Bishop" means:

   a) Servant, helper
   b) Overseer, superintendent
   c) Pastor, shepherd
   d) Preacher, teacher

4. "Pastor" means:

   a) Minister
   b) Servant
   c) Shepherd
   d) Helper

5. In 1 Timothy, Paul tells Timothy to take warning from what two false teachers?

   a) Marcion and Origen
   b) Annas and Gamaliel
   c) Simon Magus and Tertullus
   d) Hymenaeus and Alexander

6. A repeated formula in 1 Timothy is _____.

   a) "Amen, amen I say to you"
   b) "Trustworthy is the statement"
   c) "Lo and behold!"
   d) "Hear and understand"

7. Under certain guidelines, says Paul, to what class of people should a local church give financial help?

   a) Orphans
   b) Beggars
   c) Widows
   d) Widowers

8. In Titus, Paul calls Jesus's return the _____.

   a) Blessed hope
   b) Second advent
   c) Revelation of Jesus Christ
   d) End of the age

9. In 2 Timothy, Paul describes "all Scripture" as:

a) Inspired by God
b) Profitable
c) Dedicated to God
d) A & C
e) All of the above

10. "Orthopraxy" means:

a) Right belief
b) Right conduct
c) Right friendships
d) All of the above

4. The exhortation in Hebrews 10:24 to meet with fellow Christians suggests that the readers had:

   a) Split off from the main group of Christians
   b) Apostatized completely
   c) Expelled from their midst weaker Christians
   d) Been expelled from the church by discipline

5. According to Hebrews, the heavenly "rest" of Christians is symbolized in the Old Testament by _____.

   a) The tabernacle
   b) The land of Canaan
   c) The temple
   d) Jerusalem or Mt. Zion

6. The Old Testament heroes of faith are cited in Hebrews chapter _____.

   a) 1
   b) 6
   c) 10
   d) 11

7. Which of the following statements is NOT true?

   a) Hebrews presents Jesus as "better than" Melchizedek
   b) Hebrews presents Jesus as "better than" angels
   c) Hebrews presents Jesus as "better than" Moses
   d) Hebrews presents Jesus as "better than" Aaron

8. In the Greek texts of Hebrews and the Old Testament, "Jesus" is spelled the same as:

   a) Jehu
   b) Joab
   c) Joshua
   d) Jehovah

9. "Melchizedek" means:

   a) Priest of God
   b) King of righteousness

    c) Peace of the Lord

    d) Tithe

10. Which of the following statements is NOT true?

    a) Jesus's priesthood deals with heavenly realities

    b) Jesus's priesthood was instituted with a divine oath

    c) Jesus's priesthood renewed the Mosaic covenant

    d) Jesus's priesthood is based on a once-for-all sacrifice

CHAPTER 17

The Catholic, or General, Letters

You Should Know

- There are seven Catholic (i.e. "general" or "universal") letters, including: James, 1–2 Peter, 1–3 John, and Jude.

- James, the half-brother of Jesus, wrote his very practical, moral letter which offers a correct understanding of good works and complements Paul's emphasis on faith.

- James writes of justification by works *before other human beings* who need outward evidence because they *cannot* see into the heart.

- First and Second Peter are addressed to Gentiles coming under persecution in Asia Minor.

- First Peter emphasizes proper Christian conduct in the face of anti-Christian hostility and on the compensatory gift of salvation that will reach completion in the future.

- Second Peter polemicizes against heretical teachers who peddled false doctrine and practiced immorality, particularly against their denial of Jesus's return, and affirms the true knowledge of Christian belief to counter their heretical teaching.

- Jude was written by the brother of Jesus, most likely in the 50s or mid-60s, in order to encourage his congregation against false teaching.

- Jude is known for its integration of apocryphal material.

- John writes to a community in Asia Minor, perhaps in Ephesus, who were very pneumatic and afflicted by the false teachings of proto-Gnostics.

• Catholic: general, universal

Reflection Questions

1. What is "true religion" to James and how is that similar or different to our contemporary and traditional notions of religion?

2. What is the understanding of the church's relationship to Israel in 1 Peter?

3. What is the criterion for discerning whether a spirit is from God or from the Antichrist in 1 John? How does that play itself out in John's Gospel and letters?

Essay Question

1. Does James's doctrine of works contradict Paul's doctrine of faith? Explain.

Quiz

1. As applied to a group of letters, "catholic" means:
   a) Authoritative, inspired
   b) Traditional, accepted
   c) Ecclesiastical
   d) General, universal

2. Peter compares baptism to _____.
   a) The flood
   b) Israel's passage through the Red Sea
   c) Israel's passage through the Jordan River
   d) Levitical washings

3. Second Peter and Jude share the topic of _____.

a) The kingdom of God
b) Persecution
c) Eternal punishment
d) False teachers

4. In 2 Peter 3:15–16, Paul's letters are classified with "the other
_____."

a) Letters
b) Scriptures
c) Prophets
d) Logia

5. Jude quotes verbatim a passage from the pseudepigraphal, apocalyptic book of _____.

a) 1 Esdras
b) 1 Maccabees
c) 1 Baruch
d) 1 Enoch

6. James often alludes to _____.

a) The Sermon on the Mount
b) The letters of Paul
c) Semitic parts of Acts
d) 2 Peter

7. James stresses which of the following?

a) Faith as the necessary origin of good works
b) Good works as the necessary outcome of faith
c) The dichotomy or opposition of faith and good works
d) None of the above

8. In 1 John, what recurring expression suggests that John was addressing a limited group of believers well known to him?

a) "Friends"
b) "Saints"
c) "Brethren"
d) "Little children"

9. The letter with the main theme of suffering, or persecution, is _____.

    a) Hebrews
    b) 1 Peter
    c) 1 John
    d) Jude

10. Which of the following is NOT one of the three criteria of genuine Christian profession according to 1 John?

    a) Persistent prayer
    b) Righteous conduct
    c) Mutual Christian love
    d) Incarnational Christology

CHAPTER 18

Revelation

Jesus Is Coming

You Should Know

- The prophecies in the book of Revelation focus on the eschatological triumph of Christ over the anti-Christian forces of the world, all to the great encouragement of Christians who face worldly allurements and the antagonism of an unbelieving society.

- John the apostle wrote Revelation while exiled on the island of Patmos.

- John writes to Christians who are suffering for their faith in Christ between the Roman persecutions of Nero and Domitian.

- The genre of an apocalypse is characterized by revelatory literature, couched in a narrative framework that is mediated by an angel and concerns eschatological salvation.

- The Apocalypse's writing style is remarkably different from John's Gospel and letters, due to its early date, its symbolic style, and his lack of an amanuensis.

- There are a wide variety of ways that Christians have construed Revelation throughout the centuries.

- The Apocalypse: another name for the book of Revelation

- Domitian: the reigning emperor during the time of Revelation whose enforcement of worship presaged the violent persecutions to come

- Schools of interpretation: idealism, preterism, historicism, futurism

- Marriage supper: represents a uniting of the saints with their Savior at the long-awaited messianic banquet

Reflection Questions

1. How can you discern John the Apostle to be the author of Revelation? How does the Apocalypse relate to similarities and differences in John's Gospel and letters?

2. What are the differences between the idealist, preterist, historicist, and futurist interpretive schools?

3. How do other parts of Scripture clarify the child, the woman clothed with the sun, the dragon, and the marriage banquet in Revelation?

Essay Question

1. What are the differences between pretribulationism, posttribulationism, amillenialism, and premillenialism?

Quiz

1. In the writings of the early church fathers, the Johannine authorship and canonicity of Revelation were generally _____.
   a) Supported
   b) Doubted
   c) Denied
   d) Ignored

2. The book of Revelation is also called the "_____."
   a) Parousia
   b) Epiphany
   c) Apocalypse
   d) Eschatology

3. There are three series of seven plagues in Revelation. The first are called the _____.

   a) Seals
   b) Bowls
   c) Thunders
   d) Trumpets

4. The *main* purpose of Revelation is to:

   a) Reveal the future
   b) Explain the past
   c) Exhort believers to watchfulness
   d) Encourage the persecuted

5. The first series of plagues in Revelation appears to arise mainly from:

   a) Divine wrath
   b) Human wickedness
   c) Satanic-demonic activity
   d) All of the above

6. In Revelation, the New Jerusalem, which is Christ's bride, contrasts with:

   a) The old Jerusalem, where Christ was crucified
   b) The harlot Babylon, which persecuted the saints
   c) The nation of Israel, which turned out to be a faithless wife to Yahweh
   d) Sodom and Gomorrah

7. The bulk of Revelation deals with the whole of church history according to:

   a) Preterist interpretation
   b) Idealist interpretation
   c) Historicist interpretation
   d) Futurist interpretation

8. The bulk of Revelation deals with the events of the tribulation and following according to:

a) Preterist interpretation
b) Idealist interpretation
c) Historicist interpretation
d) Futurist interpretation

9. The bulk of Revelation relates to the situation of the church in the first century according to:

a) Preterist interpretation
b) Idealist interpretation
c) Historicist interpretation
d) Futurist interpretation

10. To what animal is Jesus compared in one of John's visions?

a) A lion
b) A lamb
c) Both of the above
d) Neither of the above

Notes

www.ingramcontent.com/pod-product-compliance
Lightning Source LLC
Chambersburg PA
CBHW010920040426
42445CB00017B/1934